Arthur Murphy

The apprentice

A farce. In two acts.

Arthur Murphy

The apprentice
A farce. In two acts.

ISBN/EAN: 9783741174384

Manufactured in Europe, USA, Canada, Australia, Japa

Cover: Foto ©Thomas Meinert / pixelio.de

Manufactured and distributed by brebook publishing software
(www.brebook.com)

Arthur Murphy

The apprentice

THE
APPRENTICE.

A

F A R C E.

I N

T W O   A C T S.

As it is performed at the

T H E A T R E - R O Y A L,

I N

D R U R Y - L A N E.

B Y   M R.   M U R P H Y.

L O N D O N,

Printed for P. VAILLANT. 1764.

ADVERTISEMENT.

THERE was Room to apprehend, before the Representation of the following Farce, that the Subject might appear extravagant and merely ideal; but the real Existence of it is displayed in such a lively and picturesque Manner by the Author of the Prologue, and was at once so universally felt by the Audience, that all Necessity of saying any Thing farther on this Head is now entirely superseded. What at present remains to be feared, is, that the APPRENTICE will not make so lively a Figure in the Closet, as on the Stage, where the Parts in general were allowed to be well performed; where *Simon* was represented with a Perfection of Folly; where the Skill of Mr. *Yates* exhibited the Impotence of a Mind, whose Ideas extend very little beyond the Multiplication Table, and whose Passions are ever in a crazy Conflict, unless when they all subside into a sordid Love of Gain; and where Mr. *Woodward's* admirable comic Genius gave such a Spirit to the Whole, that there is Reason to think, whenever he relinquishes the Part, the *Apprentice* may gain elope from his Friends, without any one's desiring him to return to his Business.

The Author has, however, endeavoured to render all its Defects as excuseable as he could; and he wishes no stronger Criticism could be brought against him, than the two following Observations, which he thinks very singular, and somewhat entertaining. " *I can't,* says one, *give my Opinion of the* " *Piece, till I have Time to consider the Depth of it.*"— " *Po!* says another, *this is not all his* OWN, *I re-* " *member some of it in other Plays.*"—In order to assist the former in his deep Researches, and to enable the latter to make good his Charge of Plagiarism, References are made to the several Plays, from which the distempered Hero of the Piece makes up

his

his motley, but characteriſtick Dialect. The intelligent Reader, if he thinks it worth his while to turn over theſe Leaves, will be pleaſed to remember, that a Parody does not always carry with it a Burleſque on the Lines alluded to. For (as it is judiciouſly remarked in a Note to Mr. *Pope's* Dunciad) "*It is a common, but frolick, Miſtake, that a ludicrous Parody of a grave and celebrated Paſſage, is a Ridicule of that Paſſage. A Ridicule indeed there is in every Parody: but where the Image is transferred from one Object to another, there the Ridicule falls not on the Thing* imitated, *but* imitating." Thus, for Inſtance, when

Old Edward's Armour beams on Cibber's Breaſt †,

It is without Doubt an Object ridiculous enough; but then, I think, *it falls neither on old King Edward, nor his Armour, but on his Armour-Bearer only.*

But this is prefacing a Farce, as if It were a Thing of Moment; I ſhall therefore diſmiſs It to the Preſs, without adding any Thing farther, except my grateful Acknowledgments for the very favourable Reception with which the Public has honoured the trifling Scenes of

Tavistock-Row,
5th Jan. 1756.

Their moſt obliged,
and moſt obedient Servant.

ARTHUR MURPHY,

† Line of Pope's in a ludicrous Account of the Coronation in Henry the VIIIth.

P R O

PROLOGUE

Written by Mr. GARRICK,

And spoken by Mr. WOODWARD.

PROLOGUES *precede the Piece — in mournful*
    Verse;
As Undertakers——walk before the Horse;
Whose doleful March may strike the burden'd Mind,
And wake its Feelings——for the Dead——behind.
To Night no smuggled Scenes from France we shew,
'Tis English——English, Sirs!——from Top to Toe.
Tho' coarse the Colour, and the Hand unskill'd,
From real Life our little Globe is fill'd.
The Hero is a Youth,——by Fate design'd
For culling Simples,——but whose Stage-struck Mind,
Nor Fate could rule, nor his Indentures bind.
A Place there is where such young Quixotes meet;
'Tis call'd the SPOUTING-CLUB——a glorious
    Treat!
Where 'prentic'd Kings——alarm the gaping Street!
There Brutus starts and stares by midnight Taper;
Who all the DAY enacts——a Woollen Draper.
There Hamlet's Ghost stalks forth with doubl'd Fist,
Cries out with hollow Voice,——" Lift, Lift, O Lift!"
And frightens Denmark's Prince——a young Tobacconist.
The Spirit too, clear'd from his deadly White,
Rises——a Haberdasher to the Sight!
Not young Attorneys——have this Rage withstood,
But change their Pens for TRUNCHEONS, Ink for
    BLOOD;
And (strange Reverse!)——die for their Country's Good.
  To check these Heroes, and their Laurels crop,
To bring 'em back to Reason,——and their SHOP,
Our Author wrote;—O you Tom, Dick, Jack, Will!
Who hold the Ballance, or who gild the Pill;——

Who

Wha would the Yard, and fimpering pay your Court,
And at each Flourish, faip an Inch too fhort!
Quit not your Shops; there Thrift and Profit call,
Whilft here young Gentlemen are apt to fall!
                                    [Bell rings.]
But foft!—the Prompter calls!—brief let me be—
Her Groans you'll hear, and flying Apples fee,
Be damn'd, perhaps;—farewell!—Remember me.

Dramatis Perfonæ.

Wingate, a paffionate old Man, particularly fond of Money and Figures, and involuntarily uneafy about his Son,	Mr. YATES.
Dick, his Son, bound to an Apothecary, and fond of going on the Stage,	Mr. WOOWARD.
Gargle, an Apothecary,	Mr. BURTON.
Charlotte, Daughter to Gargle,	Mifs MINORS.
Simon, Servant to Gargle,	Mr. H. VAUGHAN.
Scotchman,	Mr. BLAKES.
Irifhman,	Mr. JEFFERSON.
Catchpole, a Balliff,	Mr. VAUGHAN.

Sporting-Club, Watchmen, &c.

THE

THE

APPRENTICE.

ACT I. SCENE I.

Enter WINGATE *and* SIMON.

WINGATE.

NAY nay, but I tell you I am convinced—I know it is so,—and so, Friend, don't you think to trifle with me;—I know you're in the Plot, you Scoundrel, and if you don't discover all, I'll—

Simon. Dear Heart, Sir, you won't give a Body Time.

Wingate. Zockers! a whole Month misfing, and no Account of him far or near,—Wounds! 'tis unaccountable——Look ye, Friend,——don't you pretend——

B *Simon.*

Simon. Lord, Sir,—you're fo main paffion-
ate, you won't let a Body fpeak.

Wingate. Speak out then,—and don't ftand
muttering——What a lubberly Fellow you
are! ha! ha!——Why don't you fpeak out,
you Blockhead?

Simon. Lord, Sir, to be fure the Gentleman is a fine young Gentleman, and a fweet
young Gentleman—but, lack-a-day, Sir,—
how fhould I know any thing of him?

Wingate. Sirrah, I fay he could not be
'Prentice to your Mafter fo long, and you
live fo long in one Houfe with him, without
knowing his Haunts and all his Ways—and
then, Varlet, what brings you here to my
Houfe fo often?

Simon. My Mafter *Gargle* and I, Sir, are
fo uneafy about un, that I have been running all over the Town fince Morning to enquire for un;—and fo in my way, I thought
I might as well call here—

Wingate. A Villain, to give his Father all
this Trouble——And fo you have not heard
any Thing of him, Friend?

Simon. Not a Word, Sir, as I hope for
Marcy; tho', as fure as you are there, I believe I can guefs what's come on un.   As fure
as any thing, Mafter, the Gypfies have got-
ten hold on un, and we fhall have un come
home as thin as a Rake,—like the young
Girl in the City,—with living upon nothing
but Crufts and Water for fix-and-twenty
Days.——

Win.

Wingate. The Gypfies have got hold of him, ye Blockhead!—Get out of the Room——Here, you *Simon*——

Simon. Sir,——

Wingate. Where are you going in fuch a Hurry?——Let me fee ; what muft be done?——A ridiculous Numfkull, with his damned *Caffanders* and *Cleopatra's* and Trumpery ; with his *Romances*, and his Odyffey *Popes*, and a Parcel of Rafcals not worth a Groat ;—— wearing Stone Buckles, and cocking his Hat ; —I never wear Stone Buckles,—never cock my Hat—but, Zookers, I'll not put myfelf in a Paffion—*Simon*, do you ftep back to your Mafter, my Friend *Gargle*, and tell him I want to fpeak with him—though I don't know what I fhould fend for him for——a fly, flow, hefitating Blockhead !——he'll only plague me with his Phyfical Cant and his Nonfenfe—— Why don't you go, you Booby, when I bid you ?——

Simon. Yes, Sir—— [*Exit.*

Wingate. This Fellow will be the Death of me at laft——I can't fleep in my Bed fometimes for him. —— An abfurd infignificant Rafcal,——to ftand in his own Light !—— Death and Fury, that we can't get Children, without having a Love for 'em !—I have been turmoiling for the Fellow all the Days of my Life, and now the Scoundrel's run away—— Suppofe I advertife the Dog, and promife a Reward to any one that can give an Account of him——well, but,——why fhould I throw away my Money after him ?——, why, as I don't fay what Reward, I may give

what

what I pleafe when they come——ay, but if
the Villain fhould deceive me, and happen to
be dead,— why then he tricks me out of
Two Shillings——my Money's flung into the
Fire——Zookers, I'll not put myfelf in a
Paffion——let him follow his Nofe——'tis
nothing at all to me——what care I?——
What do you come back for, Friend?——

Re-enter Simon.

Simon. As I was going out, Sir, the Poft
came to the Door, and brought this Letter.

Wingate. Let me fee it——The Gypfies
have got hold of him! ha! ha! what a pretty
Fellow you are! ha! ha! why don't you ftep
where I bid you, Sirrah!——

Simon. Yes, Sir.   [*Exit.*

Wingate. Well, well,——I'm refolved, and
it fhall be fo——I'll advertife him To-morrow
Morning, and promife, if he comes home,
all fhall be forgiven:—And when the Blockhead comes, I may do as I pleafe——ha! ha!
I may do as I pleafe!——Let me fee:——He
had on——a Silver-loop'd Hat:——I never
liked thofe vile Silver Loops:——A Silver-
loop'd Hat;——and——and——Slidikins,
what fignifies what he had on?——I'll read
my Letter, and think no more about him.——
Hey! what a Plague have we here? [*mutters
to himfelf.*] *Briftol*——a——what's all this?——

    " *Efteemed Friend,*
    " Laft was 20th *ultimo*, fince none of
f! thine, which will occafion Brevity. The
                              " Rea-

" Reason of my writing to thee at present
" is to inform thee that thy Son came to ou
" Place with a Company of Strollers, wh
" were taken up by the Magistrate, and com
" mitted as Vagabonds, to Jail.——

Zookers! I'm glad of it——a Villain of a Fellow! Let him lie there——

" I am sorry thy Lad should follow such pro-
" fane Courses; but out of the Esteem I
" bear unto thee, I have taken thy Boy out
" of Confinement, and sent him off for your
" City in the Waggon, which left this four
" Days ago. He is consigned to thy Ad-
" dress, being the needful from thy Friend
" and Servant,

" *Ebenezer Broadbrim.*"

Wounds! what did he take the Fellow out for?——a Scoundrel, Rascal!——turn'd Stage-Player——I'll never see the Villain's Face.——Who comes there?——

Enter Simon.

Simon. I met my Master on the Way, Sir; —our Cares are over:——Here he is, Sir.——

Wingate. Let him come in——and do you go down Stairs, you Blockhead.——

[*Exit* Simon.

Enter

Enter Gargle.

Wingate. So, Friend *Gargle*,——Here's a fine Piece of Work——*Dick*'s turned Vagabond!——

Gargle. He muſt be put under a proper Regimen directly, Sir——He arrived at my Houſe within theſe ten Minutes, but in ſuch a Trim ;—He's now below Stairs—I judged it proper to leave him there, till I had prepared you for his Reception.——

Wingate. Death and Fire! what could put it into the Villain's Head to turn Buffoon?

Gargle. Nothing ſo eaſily accounted for :—— Why, when he ought to be reading the Diſpenſatory, there was he conſtantly reading over Plays, and Farces, and *Shakeſpeare.*——

Wingate. Ay, that damned *Shakeſpeare!*—— I hear the Fellow was nothing but a Deer-ſtealer in *Warwickſhire:*——Zookers! if they had hanged him out of the Way, he would not now be the Ruin of honeſt Men's Children.——But what Right had he to read *Shakeſpeare!*——I never read *Shakeſpeare!*—— Wounds! I caught the Raſcal, myſelf, reading that nonſenſical Play of *Hamblet*, where the Prince is keeping Company with Strollers and Vagabonds : A fine Example, Mr. *Gargle!*——

Gargle. His Diſorder is of the malignant Kind, and my Daughter has taken the Infection from him——bleſs my Heart!——She was as innocent as Water-gruel, till he ſpoilt her :

her :——I found her, the other Night, in the very Fact.

Wingate. Zookers! you don't fay fo !—— caught her in the Fact !—

Gargle. Ay, in the very Fact of reading a Play-book in Bed.

Wingate. O, is that the Fact you mean ?—— Is that all ?——tho' that's bad enough.——

Gargle. But I have done for my young Madam :——I have confined her to her Room, and locked up all her Books.

Wingate. Look ye, Friend *Gargle*, I'll never fee the Villain's Face :——Let him follow his Nofe and bite the Bridle.—

Gargle. Lenitives, Mr. *Wingate*——Lenitives are properest at present :——His Habit requires gentle Alteratives :—but leave him to my Management ;—about twenty Ounces of Blood, with a Cephalic Tincture,——and he may do very well.

Wingate. Where is the Scoundrel ?

Gargle. Dear Sir, moderate your Anger, and don't ufe fuch harfh Language.

Wingate. Harfh Language !——Why, do you think, Man, I'd call him a Scoundrel, if I had not a Regard for him?——You don't hear me call a Stranger a Scoundrel.

Gargle. Dear Sir, he may ftill do very well ; the Boy has very good Sentiments.——

Wingate. Sentiment !——a Fig for Sentiment ! let him get Money, and never mifs an Opportunity——I never miffed an Opportunity ; got up at Five in the Morning,— ftruck a Light,——made my own Fire—— worked my Finger's Ends——and this Va-

gabond of a Fellow is going his own Way—
with all my Heart—what care I;—let him
follow his Nofe,—let him follow his Nofe—
a ridiculous——

Gargle. Ay, ridiculous indeed, Sir—Why
for a long Time paft, he could not converfe
in the Language of common Senfe.——Afk
him but a trivial Queftion, and he'd give
fome cramp Anfwer out of fome of his Plays
that had been running in his Head, and fo
there's no underftanding a Word he fays.——

Wingate. Zookers! this comes of his keeping Company with Wits, and be damned to
'em for Wits—ha!—ha!——Wits! a fine
Thing indeed—ha! ha! 'Tis the moft beggarly, rafcally,——contemptible Thing on
Earth.——

Gargle. And then, Sir, I have found out
that he went three Times a Week to a Spouting-Club.

Wingate. A Spouting-Club, Friend *Gargle!*
—What's a Spouting-Club?

Gargle. A Meeting of 'Prentices and Clerks
and giddy young Men, intoxicated with Plays;
and fo they meet in Public-Houfes to act
Speeches; there they all neglect Bufinefs, de-
fpife the Advice of their Friends, and think of
nothing but to become Actors.——

Wingate. You don't fay fo!—a Spouting-
Club! wounds, I believe they are all mad.

Gargle. Ay, mad indeed, Sir:——Madnefs
is occafioned in a very extraordinary Manner,—
the Spirits flowing in particular Channels.——

Wingate. 'Sdeath, you're as mad yourfelf as
any of them.——

.*Gargle.*

Gargle. And continuing to run in the fame
Ducts——

Wingate. Ducks! Damn your *Ducks!*——
Who's below there?

Gargle. The Texture of the Brain becomes
diforder'd, and [Wingate *walks about uneafily,
and* Gargle *follows*] thus, by the Preffure on
the Nerves, the Head is difturbed, and fo
your Son's Malady is contracted.——

Wingate. Who's without there?——Don't
plague me fo, Man.

Gargle. But I fhall alter the morbid State
of the Juices, correct his Blood, and produce
laudable Chyle.——

Wingate. Zookers, Friend *Gargle,* don't
teaze me fo——Don't plague me with your
phyfical Nonfenfe—Who's below there?—
Tell that Fellow to come up.——

Gargle. Dear Sir, be a little cool——In-
flammatories may be dangerous.—Do, pray,
Sir, moderate your Paffions.——

Wingate. Prithee, be quiet, Man——I'll
try what I can do——Here he comes.

Enter Dick.

Dick. Now, my good Father, what's the
Matter? *

Wingate. So, Friend,——you have been
upon your Travels, have you?——You have
had your Frolic?—Look-ye, young Man,—
I'll not put myfelf in a Paffion:——But,
Death and Fire, you Scoundrel,——what

C   Right

* Hamlet.

Right have you to plague me in this Manner?——Do you think I muſt fall in Love
with your Face, becauſe I am your Father?——

Dick. A little more than Kin, and leſs than
Kind.—— •

Wingate. Ha! ha!—what a pretty Figure
you cut now?——ha! ha!——why don't
you ſpeak, you Blockhead?——Have you
nothing to ſay for yourſelf?——

Dick. Nothing to ſay for yourſelf?——
What an old Prig it is!

Wingate. Mind me, Friend——I have
found you out——I ſee you'll never come to
Good.——Turn Stage-player!——Wouads!
you'll not have an Eye in your Head in a
Month——ha! ha!——you'll have 'em
knocked out of the Sockets with withered
Apples——remember I tell you ſo.——

Dick. A Critic too! [*whiſtles*] Well done,
old Square-toes.——

Wingate. Look-ye, young Man——take
Notice of what I ſay:——I made my own
Fortune, and I could do the ſame again.
Wounds!——if I were placed at the Bottom
of *Chancery-Lane*, with a Bruſh and Black-
ball,—I'd make my own Fortune again—
you read *Shakeſpeare!*——Get *Cocker*'s *Arithmetick*—you may buy it for a Shilling on any
Stall—beſt Book that ever was wrote.——

Dick. Pretty well, that ;——Ingenious,
Faith!——Egad, the old Fellow has a
pretty Notion of Letters.

Wingate.

• Hamlet.

Wingate. Can you tell how much is *five Eighths of three Sixteenths of a Pound?*—Five Eighths of three Sixteenths of a Pound—Ay, ay, I fee you're a Blockhead :——Look-ye, young Man,—if you have a Mind to thrive in this World, ftudy Figures and make your-felf ufeful—make yourfelf ufeful.——

Dick. *How weary, ftale, flat, and unprofit-able feem to me all the Ufes of this World !——

Wingate. Mind the Scoundrel now.——

Gargle. Do, Mr. *Wingate*, let me fpeak to him——foftly, foftly——I'll touch him gently :——Come, come, young Man, lay afide this fulky Humour, and fpeak as be-comes a Son.

Dick. †O *Jeptha*, Judge of *Ifrael*, what a Treafure hadft thou !——

Wingate. What does the Fellow fay ?

Gargle. He relents, Sir——Come, come, young Man, he'll forgive.——

Dick. ‡They fool me to the Top of my Bent.——Gad, I'll hum 'em, to get rid of 'em,——a truant Difpofition, good my Lord :—— No, no, ftay, that's not right——I have a better Speech.—— " ‖ It is as you fay—when " we are fober, and reflect but ever fo little " on our Follies, we are afhamed and forry ; " and yet, the very next Minute, we rufh " again into the very fame Abfurdities."——

Wingate. Well faid, Lad, well faid—mind me, Friend : Commanding our own Paffions, and artfully taking Advantage of other People's, is the fure Road to Wealth :—Death and

---

* Hamlet.   † Ditto.   ‡ Ditto.   ‖ Sufpicious Hufband.

Fire!——but I won't put myfelf in a Paffion:——'Tis my Regard for you makes me
fpeak; and if I tell you you're a Scoundrel,
'tis for your Good.

Dick. Without Doubt, Sir. [*fiffing a Laugh.*

Wingate. If you want any Thing, you fhall
be provided:——Have you any Money in
your Pocket?—ha! ha! what a ridiculous
Numfkul you are now?—ha! ha!—Come,
here's fome Money for you.—[*Pulls out his
Money and looks at it*]—I'll give it to you another Time; and fo you'll mind what I fay
to you, and make yourfelf ufeful for the future.——

Dick. * Elfe, wherefore breathe I in a
Chriftian Land!

Wingate. Zookers! you Blockhead, you'd
better ftick to your Bufinefs, than turn Buffoon, and get Truncheons broke upon your
Arm, and be tumbling upon Carpets.——

Dick. † I fhall in all my beft obey you,
Sir.——

Wingate. Very well, Friend,——very well
faid——you may do very well if you pleafe;
and fo I'll fay no more to you, but make
yourfelf ufeful, and fo now go and clean
yourfelf, and make ready to go Home to
your Bufinefs——and mind me, young Man,
——let me fee no more Play-Books, and let
me never find that you wear a lac'd Waiftcoat——you Scoundrel, what right have
you to wear a lac'd Waiftcoat?——I never
wore a lac'd Waiftcoat!——never wore one
till

* Richard III.   † Hamlet.

till I was Forty——But I'll not put myself
in a Paſſion——go and change your Dreſs,
Friend.

    Dick. I ſhall, Sir——

    * I muſt be cruel, only to be kind,
    Thus bad begins, but worſe remains behind.'

Cocker's Arithmetick, Sir ?

    Wingate. Ay, *Cocker*'s Arithmetick——
ſtudy Figures, and they'll carry you through
the World——

    Dick. Yes, Sir, [*ſtifling a Laugh*] *Cocker*'s
Arithmetick !   [*Exit.*

Wingate *and* Gargle.

    Wingate. Let him mind me, Friend *Gargle*,
and I'll make a Man of him.

    Gargle. Ay, Sir, you know the World.——
the young Man will do very well——I wiſh
he were out of his Time ; he ſhall then have
my Daughter——

    Wingate. Yes, but I'll touch the Caſh—
he ſhan't finger it, during my Life.—I muſt
keep a tight Hand over him——[*Goes to the
Door.*]——Do ye hear, Friend !——Mind
what I ſay, and go home to your Buſineſs
immediately——Friend *Gargle*, I'll make a
Man of him.——

                          Enter

    * Hamlet.

Enter Dick.

Dick. † Who called on *Achmet*?—Did not *Barbaroffa* require me here?

Wingate. What's the Matter now?—— *Baroffa*?——Wounds!——What's *Baroffa*? ——Does the Fellow call me Names?—— What makes the Blockhead stand in such Confusion?

Dick. That *Barbaroffa* should suspect my Truth!——

Wingate. The Fellow's stark staring mad ——get out of the Room, you Villain, get out of the Room.

[*Dick stands in a sullen Mood.*

Gargle. Come, come, young Man, every Thing is easy, don't spoil all again——go and change your Dress, and come Home to your Business——nay, nay, be ruled by me
[*Thrusts him off.*

Wingate. I'm very peremptory, Friend *Gargle*; if he vexes me once more, I'll have nothing to say to him——well, but, now I think of it——I have *Cocker*'s Arithmetick below Stairs in the Counting-House——I'll step and get it for him, and so he shall take it Home with him——Friend *Gargle*, your Servant.

Gargle. Mr. *Wingate*, a good Evening to you——you'll send him Home to his Bu- siness——

Wingate.

† The last new Play called *Barbaroffa*.

Wingate. He fhall follow you Home directly. Five Eighths of three Sixteenths of a Pound! ——multiply the Numerator by the Denominator; five times Sixteen is ten times Eight, ten times Eight is Eighty, and——a ——a——carry One. [*Exit.*

Enter Dick *and* Simon.

Simon. Lord love ye, Mafter——I'm fo glad you're come back——come, we had as good e'en gang Home 'to my Mafter *Gargle's*——

Dick. No, no, *Simon*, ftay a Moment——this is but a fcurvy Coat I have on——and I know my Father has always fome Jemmy Thing lock'd up in his Clofet——I know his Ways——He takes 'em in Pawn, for he'll never part with a Shilling without Security.

Simon. Hufh! he'll hear us——ftay, I believe he's coming up Stairs.

Dick. [*Goes to the Door and liftens.*] No, no,—no,—he's going down, growling and grumbling—ay,—fay ye fo " Scoundrel, " Rafcal—Let him bite the Bridle"—" Six " times Twelve is Seventy-two"—all's fafe Man, never fear him—Do you ftand here— I fhall difpatch this Bufinefs in a Crack.——

Simon. Bleffings on him! what is he about now?—why the Door is locked, Mafter.—

Dick. Ay, but I can eafily force the Lock— you fhall fee me do it as well as any Sir *John Brute* of 'em all—this right Leg here is the

B beft

beſt Lockſmith in *England*—ſo, ſo,—[*forces the Door and goes in.*]

Simon. He's at his Plays again—Odds my Heart, he's a rare Hand—he'll go through with it, I'll warrant him—Old Cojer muſt not ſmoke that I have any Concern—I muſt be main cautious——Lord bleſs his Heart, he's to teach me to act *Scrub.*——He begun with me long ago, and I got as far as the Jeſuit before a went out of Town :——
" * Scrub—Coming, Sir,—Lord, Ma'am,
" I've a whole Packet full of News—ſome
" ſay one Thing and ſome ſay another ; but,
" for my Part, Ma'am,——I believe he's a
" Jeſuit"—that's main pleaſant—" *I believe*
" *he's a Jeſuit.*"

Re-enter Dick.

Dick. † I have done the Deed—Didſt thou not hear a Noiſe ?

Simon. No, Maſter ; we're all ſnug.—

Dick. This Coat will do charmingly—I have bilked the old Fellow nicely——‡ In a dark Corner of his Cabinet, I found this Paper ; what it is the Light will ſhew.

I promiſe to pay——ha !——

I promiſe to pay to Mr. *Moneytrap,* or Order, on Demand—'tis *his Hand*—*a Note of his*—*yet more*—The Sum of ſeven Pounds fourteen Shillings and Seven Pence, Value received, by me

London this 15th *June,* 1755.——'Tis wanting what ſhould follow——*his* Name ſhould

fol-

* *Stratagem.* † *Macbeth.* ‡ *Vide* the Mourning Bride.

follow—but 'tis torn off—becaufe the Note is paid.——

Simon. O Lud! Dear Sir, you'll fpoil all— I wifh we were well out of the Houfe—Our beft Way, Mafter, is to make off direCtly.—

Dick. I will, I will; but firft help me on with this Coat——*Simon,* you fhall be my Dreffer—you'll be fine and happy behind tho Scenes.——

Simon. O Lud! it will be main pleafant—I have been behind the Scenes in the Country, when I liv'd with the Man that fhew'd wild Beaftices.——

Dick. Hark-ye, *Simon,*—when I am playing fome deep Tragedy, and * cleave the general Ear with horrid Speech, you muft ftand between the Scenes and cry bitterly.[*Teaches him.*

Simon. Yes, Sir.

Dick. And when I'm playing Comedy, you muft be ready to laugh your Guts out [*Teaches him.*] for I fhall be very pleafant——Tolderoll—[*Dances.*]

Simon. Never doubt me, Sir.——

Dick. Very well; now run down and open the Street-Door; I'll follow you in a Crack.

Simon. I am gone to ferve you, Mafter.——

Dick. † To ferve theyfelf——for, look-ye, *Simon,* when I am Manager, claim thou of me the Care o'th' Wardrobe, with all thofe Moveables, whereof the § Property-Man now ftands poffeft.——

D

Simon.

---

* Hamlet.   † Richard III.
§ The Property-Man, in the Play-Houfe Phrafe, is the Perfon who gives Truncheons, Daggers, &c. to the Actors, as Occafion requires.

Simon. O Lud! this is charming—Hush! I am gone.   [*Going.*

Dick. Well, but hark-ye, *Simon*, come hither——* what Money have you about you, Master *Matthew*?

Simon. But a Tester, Sir.

Dick. A Tester!———That's something of the least, Master *Matthew*,——let's see it.

Simon. You have had fifteen Sixpences now——

Dick. Never mind that——I'll pay you all at my Benefit——

Simon. I don't doubt that, Master——— but mum.   [*Exit.*

Dick, *solus.*

† Thus far we run before the Wind.—— An Apothecary!——make an Apothecary of me!——‡ what, cramp my Genius over a Pestle and Mortar, or mew me up in a Shop with an Alligator stuft, and a beggarly Account of empty Boxes!——to be culling Simples, and constantly adding to the Bills of Mortality,——No! no! It will be much better to be pasted up in Capitals, *The Part of Romeo by a young Gentleman, who never appeared on any Stage before!*——My Ambition fires at the Thought——But hold, ——mayn't I run some Chance of failing in

* Every Man in his Humour.   † Richard III.
‡ *Vide* Romeo and Juliet.

In my Attempt——Hiffed,——Pelted,——
Laughed at,——Not admitted into the Green-
Room——That will never do—— *Down,
bufy Devil, down, down.—Try it again.—
Loved by the Women, envied by the Men,
applauded by the Pit, clapped by the Gallery,
admired by the Boxes. " Dear Colonel, is not
" he a charming Creature ?" " My Lord,
" don't you like him of all Things ?"——
" Makes Love like an Angel !"——" What
" an Eye he has!——fine Legs !"——
" I'll certainly go to his Benefit."——Ce-
leftial Sounds!——And then I'll get in
with all the Painters, and have myfelf put
up in every Print-Shop—in the Character of
Macbeth ! " This is a forry Sight." [*ftands an
Attitude.*] In the Character of *Richard* [*Give
me another Horfe, bind up my Wounds.*]——
this will do rarely——and then I have a
Chance of getting well married——O
glorious Thought!——† By Heaven I will
enjoy it, though but in Fancy—— But,
what's o'Clock ?——it muft be almoft Nine.
I'll away at once ; this is Club-night.——
'Egad I'll go to 'em for a while——the
Spouters are all met——little they think
I'm in Town——they'll be furprifed to
fee me——Off I go, and then for my Af-
fignation with my Mafter *Gargle*'s Daughter
——Poor *Charlotte !*——fhe's lock'd up,
but I fhall find Means to fettle Matters for
her Efcape——She's a pretty Theatrical

　　　　　　　D 2　　　　　　Genius

* Venice Preferv'd.　　† Tamerlane.

Genius——If she flies to my Arms like a
Hawk to its Perch, it will be so rare an Adventure, and so Dramatic an Incident,——

* Limbs do your Office, and support me well;
Bear me but to her, then fail me if you can.

       • The Orphan.

E N D of the F I R S T   A C T.

A C T

ACT II. SCENE I.

Scene discovers the Spouting-Club, the Members seated and roaring out Bravo, *while one stands at a Distance repeating*————

1st. Member. CURS'D be your Senate, curs'd your Constitution; The Curse of growing Factions and Divisions Still vex your Councils.*————

2d. Memb. Don't you think his Action a little confined ?

1st. Memb. Psha ! you Blockhead, don't you know that I'm in Chains ?——

2d. Memb. Blockhead, say ye ?——Was not I the first that took Compassion on you, when you lay like a sneaking Fellow under the Counter, and swept your Master's Shop in a Morning ? when you read nothing but the *Young Man's Pocket Companion*, or the *True Clerk's Vade Mecum*, did not I put *Chrononbotonthologos* in your Hand ?

All. Bravo ! Bravo !——

President. Come, Gentlemen, let us have no Disputes. Consider, Gentlemen, this is the Honourable Society of Spouters ; and so, to put an End to all Animosities, read the seventh Rule of this Society.

A Mem-

* *Venice Preserv'd.*

A Member Reads,

" *That Bufinefs, or Want of Money, fhall not*
" *be received as an Excufe for Non-Attendance;*
" *nor the Anger of Parents or other Relations;*
" *nor the Complaints of our Mafters be ever heard;*
" *by which Means this Society will be able to boaft*
" *its own mimic Heroes, and be a Nurfery of*
" *Young* Actorlings *for the Stage, in Spight of*
" *the Mechanic Genius of our Friends.*"

Prefident. That is not the Rule I mean;—
but come, * we'll fill a Meafure the Table
round—now good Digeftion wait on Appetite,
and Health on both.

All. Huzza, huzza, huzza!——

Prefident. Come, Gentlemen, let us have
no Quarrels.

All. Huzza, huzza!——

Scotchman. Come now I'll gee you a Touch
of *Macbeeth.*——

1ft. Memb. That will be rare. Come let's
have it.——

Scotchman. What do'ft lier at Mon?—I have
had muckle Applaufe at *Edinburgh,* when I
enacted in the *Regiceede,*—and I now intend
to do *Macbeeth*—I feed the *Degger* Yefterneet,
and I thought I fhould ha' killed every one
that came in my Way.—

Irifhman. Stand out of the way, Lads, and
you'll fee me give a Touch of *Otbello,* my Dear—
[*Takes the Cork and burns it, and blacks his Face.*]
The Devil burn the Cork—it would not do it
faft enough.

1ft.

* Macbeth.

1*ß. Memb.* Here, here, I'll lend you a helping Hand. [*Blacks him.*]

[*Knocking at the Door.*]

2*d. Memb.* *Open Locks, whoever knocks.—

Enter Dick.

Dick. † How now, ye Secret, Black, and Midnight Hags?—what is't ye do?

All. Ha! the Genius come to Town—Huzza! huzza!—the Genius—

Dick. How fare the honest Partners of my Heart?—*Jack Hopeless,* give us your Hand—*Guildcrßen,* yours—Ha! *Rosencrofs*—Gentlemen, I rejoice to see ye—But come, the News, the News of the Town!—Has any Thing been damned?—Any new Performers this Winter?—How often has *Romeo* and *Juliet* been acted?—Come, my Bucks, inform me, I want News.—

1*ß. Memb.* You shall know all in good Time—But prithee, my dear Boy, how was it?—You play'd at *Bristol,* let's hear.—

2*d. Memb.* Ay, let's have it, dear *Dick.*—

Dick. Look-ye there now—‡ Let's have it, dear Boy, and dear *Dick.*——

1*ß. Memb.* Nay, nay, but how was you receiv'd?—

Dick. Romeo was my Part——I touch'd their Souls for 'em,—every pale Face from the Wells was there, and so on I went—but rot 'em,—never mind them— ‖ What bloody Scene has *Roscius* now to act?—

1*ß.*

* *Macbeth.*   † Ditto.   ‡ Suspicious Husband.
‖ R.chard III.   2

1ſt. Memb. Several Things—But, Genius, why did you come to us ſo late ?—Why did not you come in the Beginning of the Night?

Dick. Why, I intended it : But who ſhould I meet in my Way but by Friend *Catcall*, a devilish good Critic ;—and ſo he and I went together and had our Pipes, to ʼcloſe the Orifice of the Stomach you know ;—and what do you think I learn'd of him ?

1ſt. Memb. I can't ſay.

Dick. Can you tell, now, whether the Emphaſis ſhould be laid upon the *Epitaph*†, or the *Subſtantive?*

1ſt. Memb. Why, no.——

Dick. Ever, while you live, lay your Emphaſis upon the *Epitaph*.——

Iriſhman. Arrah, my Dear, but what is that ſame Epitaph now ?

Dick. ‡ Arrah, my dear Couſin *Mackſhane*, won't you put a Remembrance upon me ?—

Iriſhman. Ow ! but is it mocking you are ? —Look-ye, my Dear, if you'd be taking me off—Don't you call it taking off ?—By my Shoul I'd be making you take yourſelf off——What ? If you're for being obſtropolous, I would not matter you three Skips of a Flea.——

Dick. Nay, prithee, no Offence—I hope we ſhall be Brother-players.

Iriſhman. Ow ! then we'd be very good Friends ; for you know two of a Trade can never agree, my Dear.

Scotchman.

---

* Every Man in his Humour.
† By Miſtake for *Epitaſt*.   ‡ Stratagem.

Scotchman. Locks is certainly reet in his Chapter aboot innate Ideas; for this Mon is born without any at all—and the other Mon yonder, I doot, is no greet Heed-piece.——

Dick. What do you intend to appear in?

Irishman. Othollo, my Dear; let me alone; you'll see how I'll *bodder* 'em—Tho' by my Shoul, myshelf does not know but I'd be frightened when every Thing is in a *Hub-bub,* and nothing to be heard, but "*Throw him* " *over*"—" *over with him*"—" off, off, off the " *Stage*"—" *Music*"—" *Won't* y' *ba'* some " *Orange-chips*"——" *won't* y' *ba'* some *Non-* " *pareills ?*"——Ow!—but may-be the dear Craturs in the Boxes will be *lucking* at my Legs—Ow! to be sure——the Devil burn the *Luck* they'll give 'em.——

Dick. I shall certainly laugh in the Fellow's Face.——

Irishman. Ow I never mind it——let me alone, my Dear——may-be I'd see a little round Face from *Dublin* in the Pit, may-be I wou'd; but then, won't I be the first Gentleman of my Name that turn'd Stage-play'r?— My Cousins would rather see me starve like a Gentleman, with Honour and Reputation— Myshelf does be asham'd when I think of it.—

Scotchman. Stay till you hear me give a Speecimen of Elocution.

Dick. What, with that Impediment, Sir?

Scotchman. Impeediment! what Impeediment? I do not leesp——do I?——I do no squeent——I am well leem'd, am I not?——

Irishman. By my Shoul, if you go to that, I am as well timber'd myself as any of them,

E   and

and fhall make a Figure in genteel and top Comedy.——

Scotchman. I'll give you a Speecimen of *Mockbeeth.*————

Irifhman. Make hafte, then, and I'll begin *Othello.*————

Scotchman. ——Is this a Dagger that I fee before me, &c.

Irifhman. [*collaring bim.*] * Willain, be fure you prove my Love a Whore, &c.

[*Another Member comes forward with bis Face powdered, and a Pipe in bis Hand.*]

——I am thy Father's Spirit, *Hamlet*——

Dick. Po! Prithee! you're not fat enough for a Ghoft.——

Memb. I intend to make my firft Appearance in it for all that, only I'm puzzled about one Thing——I want to know, when I come on firft, whether I fhould make a Bow to the Audience?

Another Memb. Now, Gentlemen, for the true way of dying——[*fpreads a Blanket.*]—— now for a little Phrenzy——[*Repeats a dying Speech, and rolls bimfelf up in the Blanket.*]——

[*Watch behind the Scenes ; Paft Five o'Clock, cloudy Morning.*]

Dick. Hey! paft Five o'Clock——'Sdeath, I fhall mifs my Appointment with *Charlotte*—— I have ftaid too long, and fhall lofe my Profelyte——Come, let us adjourn.——

All. Ay, let us fally forth.——

Irifhman. With all my Heart; tho' I fhould have bodder'd 'em finely if they had ftaid.

Scotch-

* *Venice Preferv'd.*

Scotchman. I fhould have fheen'd in *Mockbeeth*————but never meend it————I'll go
now to my Friend the Bookfeller, and tranf-
late *Cornelius Tacitus*, or *Gretius de Jure Belli*,
————and fo, Gentlemen, your Servant.——

All. Huzza! Huzza!

Dick. * We'll fcower the Watch————Con-
fufion to Morality——I wifh the Conftable
were married——Huzza, Huzza——

Irifhman. By my Shoul, myfhelf did not
care if I had a Wife, with a good Fortune, to
be hindering me from going on——But no
matter——I may meet with a willing Cratur
fomewhere——   [*Exit finging.*

All. Huzza, Huzza!——   [*Exeunt.*

SCENE, *a Street.*

Enter a Watchman.

Paft Five o'Clock, cloudy Morning. Mercy
on us——all mad I believe in this Houfe—
They're at this Trade three Nights in the
Week, I think————Paft Five o'Clock, a
cloudy Morning.

All. Huzza! [*without.*]

Watchman. What in the Name of Wonder
are they all at?

Hurra, Hurra, without. Enter the Spouters.

Dick. † Angels and Minifters of Grace de-
fend us!

E 2   1*ft. Memb.*

* Sir John Brute.   † Hamlet.

1β. *Memb.* * By Heavens I'll tear you Joint by Joint, and ftrew this hungry Church-yard with your Limbs.

Dick. † Avant, and quit my Sight——thy Bones are marrowlefs————There's no Speculation in thofe Eyes, that thou doft glare withal.

Watchman. Prithee don't diftrub the Peace——

A Member. ‡ Be fure you write him down an Afs.

Dick. § Be alive again, and dare me to the Defart with thy Pole,————take any Shape but that, and my firm Nerves fhall never tremble————

Watchman. Soho! Soho!

Enter Watchmen from all Parts, fome drunk, fome coughing, &c.

2d. *Watchman.* What's the Matter there?——

1β. *Watchman.* Here are the Difturbers of the Peace——I charge 'em all——

Dick. ‖ Unmanner'd Slave, advance your Halbert bigher than my breaft, or by St. *Paul,* I'll ftrike thee down, and fpurn thee, Beggar, for this Infolence——

[*They fight,* Dick *is knocked down.* Exeunt *Watchmen fighting the reft.*

Dick. ** I have it, it will do,——'Egad, I'll make my Efcape now——O I am For-tune's Fool——-.   [*Exit.*
                                      Re-

* Romeo.   † Macbeth.   ‡ Much ado about Nothing.   § Macbeth.   ‖ Richard.
** Romeo.

Re-enter Watchmen, &c.

Watchman. Come, bring 'em along——
1*ft. Memb.* * Good Ruffians, hold a while—
2*d. Memb.* † I am unfortunate, but not
afhamed of being fo.
Watchman. Come, come, bring 'em along.
　　　　　　　　　　　　　　[*Exeunt.*

SCENE, *another Street.*

Enter Dick, *with a Lanthorn and a Ladder.*

All's quiet here ; the Coaft's clear ;—now
for my Adventure with *Charlotte*—this Ladder
will do rarely for the Bufinefs—tho' it would
be better, if it were a Ladder of Ropes—
but hold ; have not I feen fomething like this
on the Stage ?—yes I have, in fome of the
Entertainments —Ay, ‡ I remember an Apothecary, and hereabout he dwells—this is my
Mafter *Gargle's* ;—being dark the Beggar's
Shop is fhut—what, ho ! Apothecary !—but
foft,—what Light breaks thro' yonder Window
—It is the Eaft, and *Juliet* is the Sun ; arife
fair Sun, *&c.*
　　Charlotte. Who's there ? my *Romeo ?*
　　Dick. The fame, my Love, if it not thee
difpleafe.——
　　Charlotte. Hufh ! not fo loud, you'll waken
my Father.—
　　Dick. § Alas ! there's more peril in thy Eye.
　　　　　　　　　　　　　　　　Char-

* Revenge.　† Oroonoko.　‡ Romeo.　§ Romeo.

Charlotte. Nay, but prithee now—I tell you you'll spoil all—what made you stay so long?

Dick. *Chide not, my Fair, but let the God of Love laugh in thy Eyes, and revel in thy Heart.——

Charlotte. As I am a living Soul, you'll ruin every Thing; be but quiet, and I'll come down to you.—— [*Going.*

Dick. No, no, not so fast—*Charlotte*—let us act the Garden Scene first——

Charlotte. A Fiddlestick for the Garden Scene——

Dick. Nay, then I'll act *Ranger*—up I go, Neck or nothing.

Charlotte. Dear Heart, you're enough to frighten a Body out of one's Wits—Don't come up—I tell you there's no Occasion for the Ladder—I have settled every Thing with *Simon*, and he's to let me thro' the Shop, when he opens it.

Dick. Well, but I tell you I would not give a Farthing for it without the Ladder, and so, up I go.

Enter Simon *at the Door.*

Simon. Sir, Sir, Madam, Madam——

Dick. Prithee be quiet, *Simon*——I am ascending the high Top-gallant of my Joy—

Simon. An't please you, Master, my young Mistress may come thro' the Shop——I am going to sweep it out, and she may escape that way fast enow-——

Char-

* Fair Penitent.

Charlotte. That will do purely——and so do you stay where you are, and prepare to receive me——   [*Exit from above.*

Dick. No, no, but that won't take—you shan't hinder me from going thro' my Part [*goes up*] * a Woman, by all that's lucky— neither old nor crooked————in I go—— [*goes in*] and for Fear of the Pursuit of the Family, I'll make sure of the Ladder.

Simon. Hist! hist! Master——leave that there, to save me from being suspected——

Dick. With all my Heart, Simon——
                              [*Exit from above.*

Simon alone. Lord love him, how comical he is!——it will be fine for me, when we're playing the Fool together, to call him Brother *Martin.* " † Brother *Martin.*"

Enter Charlotte.

Charlotte. O Lud! I'm frighted out of my Wits, where is he?——

Simon. He's a coming, Ma'am——[*calls to him*] " Brother *Martin.*"

Enter Dick.

Dick. ‡ Cuckold him, Ma'am, by all Means ——I'm your Man.

Charlotte. Well now, I protest and vow, I wonder how you can serve a Body so———— feel with what a Pit-a-pat Action my Heart beats——

                                        Dick.

Dick. * 'Tis an Alarm to Love——quick
let me snatch thee to thy *Romeo's* Arms, &c.

Watchman behind the Scenes. Past Six o'Clock,
and a cloudy Morning——

Charlotte. Dear Heart, don't let us stand
fooling here——as I live and breathe we shall
both be taken——do, for Heaven's Sake, let
us make our Escape.

Watch. Past Six o'Clock, a cloudy Morning——

Charlotte. It comes nearer and nearer, let
us make off——

Dick. Give us your Hand then——my
pretty little Adventurer I attend you.
†Yes, my dear *Charlotte*, we will go together,
  Together to the Theatre we'll go,
  There to their ravish'd Eyes our Skill
      we'll show,
  And point new Beauties--to the Pit below.

Simon. Heavens bless the Couple of 'em;
but mum.
          [*Exit, and shuts the Doors after him.*

        Enter Bailiff and his Follower.

Bailiff. That's he yonder, as sure as you're
alive—Ay, it is—and he has been about some
Mischief here.

Follower. No, no, that an't he—that one
wears a laced Coat—tho' I can't say—as sure
as a Gun, it is he——

Bailiff. Ay, I smoked him at once——Do
you run that Way and stop at the Bottom of
                                    Ca-

* Old Batchelor.   † *Vide* Distress'd Mother.

Catherine-Street; I'll go up *Drury-Lane*, and between us both, it will be odds if we miss him. *[Exeunt.*

Enter Watchman.

Watch. Paſt Six a Clock, and a cloudy Morning——Hey-day! what's here, a Ladder, at Maſter *Gargle*'s Window?——I muſt alarm the Family——Ho! Maſter *Gargle*— *[Knocks at the Door.*

Gargle, above. What's the Matter?—How comes this Window to be open?——ha!—— a Ladder!——Who's below there?

1ſt. Watch. I hope you an't robbed, Maſter *Gargle?*——As I was going my Rounds, I found your Window open.

Gargle. I fear this is ſome of that young Dog's Tricks——Take away the Ladder; I muſt enquire into all this.—— *[Exit.*

Enter Simon, *like* Scrub.

Simon. • Thieves! Murder! Thieves! Popery!—

Watch What's the Matter with the Fellow?

Simon. Spare all I have, and take my Life——

Watchman. Any Miſchief in the Houſe?

Simon. They broke in with Fire and Sword ——they'll be here this Minute——Five and Forty——*This will do charmingly*—— " *my young Maſter taught me this.*" *[Aſide.*

F *1ſt.*

* *Vide* Stratagem.

1st. Watchman. What, are there Thieves in the House?

Simon. With Sword and Pistol, Sir,——Five and Forty.

Watch. Nay, then 'tis Time for me to go,——for, mayhap, I may come to ha' the worst on't—— [*Exit Watchman.*

Enter Gargle.

Gargle. Dear Heart! dear Heart——she's gone, she's gone———my Daughter! my Daughter!——what's the Fellow in such a Fright for?

Simon. Down on your Knees——down on your Marrowbones———(this will make him think, I know nothing of the Matter——Bless his Heart for teaching me)——Down on your Marrowbones.——

Gargle. Get up, you Fool, get up——Dear Heart, I'm all in a Fermentation.

Enter Wingate *reading a News-Paper.*

" Wanted, on good Security, Five hundred
" Pounds, for which lawful Interest will be
" given, and a good Præmium allowed:
" Whoever this may suit, Enquire for S. T.
" at the *Crown and Rolls* in *Chancery-Lane.*"——
This may be worth looking after.—I'll have a good Præmium—If the Fellow's a Fool, I'll fix my Eye on him—Other People's Follies are an Estate to the Man that knows how to make himself useful—So, Friend *Gargle,*——you're up early, I see——nothing like rising

early

early——nothing to be got by lying in Bed,
like a lubberly Fellow—What's the Matter
with you?—ha! ha! you look like a—ha!
ha!—

Gargle. O—no Wonder—My Daughter,
my Daughter!

Wingate. Your Daughter!—what fignifies
a foolifh Girl?

Gargle. Oh dear Heart! dear Heart!——
out of the Window.

Wingate. Fallen out of the Window!——
well, fhe was a Woman, and 'tis no Matter—
if fhe's dead, fhe's provided for.——Here,
I found the Book——could not meet with
it laft Night——Here it is——there's more
Senfe in it, than in all their *Macbeths* and
their Trumpery [*reads*] *Cocker's* Arithmetick
——Look ye here now, Friend *Gargle*,——
fuppofe you have the Sixteenth Part of a
Ship, and I buy one Fifth of you, what Share
of the Ship do I buy?——

Gargle. Oh dear, Sir, 'tis a melancholy
Cafe——

Wingate. A melancholy Cafe indeed to be
fo ignorant——why fhould not a Man
know every Thing? One Fifth of one Sixteenth, what Part have I of the Whole? Let
me fee—I'll do it a fhort Way.——

Gargale. Loft beyond Redemption.——

Wingate. Zookers, be quiet Man, you put
me out—Seven times Seven is Forty-nine,
and Six times Twelve is Seventy-two,——
and—and—and—a—Here, Friend *Gargle*,
take the Book, and give it that Scoundrel of a
Fellow.——

Gargle. Lord, Sir,—He's returned to his Tricks.——

Wingate. Returned to his Tricks!—What, —broke loose again?——

Gargle. Ay, and carried off my Daughter with him.——

Wingate. Carried off your Daughter—— How did the Rafcal contrive that?

Gargle. Oh, dear Sir,————the Watch alarmed us a while ago, and I found a Ladder at the Window——fo I fuppofe my young Madam made her Efcape that Way.—

Wingate. Wounds! what Bufinefs had the Fellow with your Daughter?

Gargle. I wifh I had never taken him into my Houfe—He may debauch the poor Girl—

Wingate. And fuppofe he does————fhe's a Woman, an't fhe?—Ha! ha! Friend *Gargle,* Ha! ha!——

Gargle. Dear Sir, how can you talk thus to a Man diftracted?

Wingate. I'll never fee the Fellow's Face.

Simon. Secrets! Secrets! *

Wingate. What, are you in the Secret, Friend?——

Simon. To be fure, there be Secrets in all Families——but, for my Part, I'll not fpeak a Word *pro* or *con,* till there's a Peace.

Wingate. You won't fpeak, Sirrah!—I'll make you fpeak——Do you know nothing of this Numfkull?

Simon. Who I, Sir?——He came home laft Night from your Houfe, and went out again directly.——

Wingate.

* *Vide* Stratagem.   z

Wingate. You faw him then—

Simon. Yes, Sir—faw him to be fure, Sir—
he made me open the Shop Door for him—
he ftopp'd on the Threfhold and pointed at
one of the Clouds, and afked me if it was not
like an *Ouzel* *?—

Wingate. Like an *Ouzel*—Wounds! what's
an *Ouzel?*——

Gargle. And the young Dog came back in
the Dead of Night to fteal away my Daughter.

Wingate. I'll tell you what, Friend *Gargle*—
I'll think no more of the Fellow—let him bite
the Bridle—I'll go mind my Bufinefs, and not
mifs an Opportunity.

Gargle. Good now, Mr. *Wingate*, don't leave
me in this Affliction,—confider, when the
animal Spirits are properly employed, the
whole Syftem's exhilarated, a proper Circu-
lation in the fmaller Ducts or Capillary Vef-
fels——

Wingate. Look-ye there now—the Fellow's
at his *Ducks* again, ha! ha!

Gargle. But when the Spirits are under In-
fluence——

Wingate. Ha! ha! what a fine fellow you
are now?—you're as mad with your phyfical
Nonfenfe, as my Son with his *Shakefpeare* and
Ben Thompfon——

Gargle. Dear Sir, let us go in queft of him
—he fhall be well phlebotomized; and for
the future I'll keep his Solids and Fluids in
proper Balance—

Wingate. Don't tell me of your Solids—
I tell you he'll never be folid—and fo I'll go
and

* Hamlet.

and mind my Bufinefs——let me fee where
is this Chap——[*reads*] ay, ay, at the *Crown
and Rolls*———good Morning, Friend *Gargle*——don't plague yourfelf about the Numfkull——ftudy Fractions Man; Vulgar Fractions will carry you through the World, Arith-
metical Proportion is when the Antecedent
and Confequent,——a——   [*going.*

Enter a Porter.

Wingate. Who are you, pray?—what do
you want?——
    Porter. Is one Mr. *Gargle* here?
    Gargle. Yes——who wants him?——
    Porter. Here's a Letter for you?——
    Gargle. Let me fee it. O dear Heart!—
[*reads*] *To Mr.* Gargle *at the Peftle and Mortar*
——'Slidikins, this is a Letter from that unfortunate young Fellow——
    Wingate. Let me fee it, *Gargle*—
    Gargle. A Moment's Patience, good Mr.
Wingate, and this may unravel all—[*reads*]—
Poor young Man!——his Brain is certainly
turned——I can't make Head or Tale of
it——
    Wingate. Ha! ha!—you're a pretty Fel-
low—give it me, Man—I'll make it out for
you—'tis his Hand fure enough [*reads*]
        To Mr. Gargle, &c.
  " *Moft Potent, Grave*[*] *and Reverend Doctor,*
  " *my very noble and approv'd good Mafter, that*
  " *I have ta'en away your Daughter it is moft*
  " *true, true I will marry her;*—†'*tis true 'tis*
                              " *Pity,*

        * Othello.   † Hamlet.

" *Pity, and Pity 'tis, 'tis true.*"——What in
the Name of Common Senfe is all this ? " * *I*
" *have done your Shop fome Service, and you*
" *know it; no more of that——yet I could wifh,*
" *that at this Time, I had not been this Thing*
——What can the Fellow mean ?——" *For*
" *Time I may have yet one fated Hour to come,*
" *which, wing'd with Liberty, may overtake Oc-*
" *cafion paft*"——overtake Occafion paft !——
Time and Tide waits for no Man——" § *I ex-*
" *pect Redrefs from thy noble Sorrows——thine*
" *and my poor Country's ever.*" R. Wingate.

Mad as a *March* Hare ! I have done with
him——let him ftay till the Shoe pinches, a
crack-brained Numfkull !

Porter. An't pleafe ye, Sir, I fancys the
Gentleman is a little befide himfelf——
he took hold un me here by the Collar, and
called me Villain **, and bid me prove his Wife
a Whore——Lord help him, I never fee'd
the Gentleman's Spoufe in my born Days before.

Gargle. Is fhe with him now ?

Porter. I believe fo——There's a likely
young Woman with him, all in Tears.——

Gargle. My Daughter to be fure——

Wingate. Let the Fellow go and be hang'd
——Wounds ! I would not go the Length of
my Arm to fave the Villain from the Gallows.
Where was he, Friend, when he gave you this
Letter ?——

Porter. I fancy, Mafter, the Gentleman's
under

---

under Troubles————I brought it from a
Spunging-House.

Wingate. From a Spungging-House!

Porter. Yes, Sir, in *Grays-Inn-Lane.*

Wingate. Let him lie there, let him lie
there——I am glad of it——

Gargle. Do, my dear Sir, let us step to
him——

Wingate. No, not I, let him stay there—
this it is to have a Genius——ha! ha!——
a Genius!——ha! ha!——a Genius is a fine
Thing indeed!——ha! ha!   [*Exit.*

Gargle. Poor Man! he has certainly a Fever
on his Spirits—do you step in with me, honeft
Man, till I flip on my Coat, and then I'll go
after this unfortunate Boy.

Porter. Yes, Sir,—'tis in *Grays-Inn-Lane.*
                                   [*Exeunt.*

Scene a Spunging-House, Dick *and* Bailiff *at a
Table, and* Charlotte *fitting in a difconfolate
Manner by him.*

Bailiff. Here's my Service to you, young
Gentleman————Don't be uneafy————the
Debt is not much——why do you look fo
fad?——

Dick. Becaufe * Captivity has robb'd me
of a juft and dear Diverfion.

Bailiff. Never look fulky at me—I never
ufe any Body ill—Come, it has been many
a good Man's Lot——here's my Service to
you—but we've no Liquor—come we'll
have t'other Bowl——

                                   Dick.

* Mourning Bride.

Dick. * I've now not Fifty Ducats in the World—yet still I am in Love, and pleas'd with Ruin.——

Bailiff. What do you say?—you've Fifty Shillings, I hope.——

Dick. † Now, thank Heaven! I'm not worth a Groat.——

Bailiff. Then there's no Credit here, I can tell you that——you must get Bail, or go to *Newgate*——who do you think is to pay House-rent for you?—You see your Friends won't come near you——They've all an-swered in the old Cant——" *I've promised* " *my Wife never to be Bail for any Body*;" or, " *I've sworn not to do it*"—or, " *I'd lend* " *you the Money if I had it, but desire to be ex-* " *cused from bailing any Man.*"—The Porter you just now sent, will bring the same An-swer, I warrant.——Such Poverty-struck Devils as you shan't stay in my House—— you shall go to *Quod*, I can tell you that—

[*Knocking at the Door.*

Bailiff. Coming, coming, I am coming—I shall lodge you in *Newgate*, I promise you, before Night——not worth a Groat!——you're a fine Fellow to stay in a Man's House ——You shall go to *Quod.*   [*Exit.*

Dick. Come, clear up, *Charlotte*, never mind this——come, now——let us act the Prison-Scene in the *Mourning Bride*——

Charlotte. How can you think of acting Speeches, when we're in such Distress?——

Dick. Nay, but my dear Angel——

G   *Enter*

---

* *Venice Preserv'd.*   † *Ditto.*

Enter Wingate *and* Gargle.

Gargle. Hufh ! Do, dear Sir, let us liften to
him—I dare fay he repents——
Wingate. Wounds !——what Cloaths are
thofe the Fellow has on ?——Zookers, the
Scoundrel has robbed me.——
Dick. Come, now we'll practife an Atti-
tude—How many of 'em have you ?——
Charlotte. Let me fee—one—two—three—
and then in the fourth Act, and then——O
Gemini, I have ten at leaft——
Dick. That will do fwimmingly——I've a
round Dozen *myfelf*—Come now begin——
you fanfy me dead, and I think the fame of
you—now mind——   [*They ftand in Attitudes.*
Wingate. Only mind the Villain.—
Dick. O thou foft fleeting Form of *Linda-
mira !*—
·*Charlotte.* * Illufive Shade of my beloved
Lord !
Dick. † She lives, fhe fpeaks, and we fhall
ftill be happy.——
Wingate. You lie, you Villain, you fhan't
be happy.—   [*Knocks him down.*
Dick. [*on the Ground.*] ‡ Perdition catch
your Arm, the Chance is thine.—
Gargle. So, my young Madam—I have
found you again.——
Dick. ‖ *Capulet* forbear; *Paris* let loofe your
Hold—She is my Wife——our Hearts are
twined together.——   *Wingate.*

* Romeo and Juliet.   † Ditto.   ‡ Richard III.
‖ Romeo.   2

Wingate. Sirrah! Villain! I'll break every Bone in your Body— [*Strikes.*

Dick. * Parents have flinty Hearts, no Tears can move 'em: Children must be wretched—

Wingate. Get off the Ground, you Villain; get off the Ground.——

Dick. 'Tis a Pity there are no Scene-drawers to lift me——

Wingate. A Scoundrel, to rob your Father; you Rascal, I've a Mind to break your Head.

Dick. † What, like this? [*Takes off his Wig, and shews two Patches on his Head.*]

Wingate. 'Tis mighty well, young Man—Zookers! I made my own Fortune; and I'll take a Boy out of the *Blue-coat-Hospital,* and give him all I have.—Look-ye here, Friend *Gargle.*—You know I'm not a hard-hearted Man—The Scoundrel, you know, has robbed me; so, d'ye see, I won't hang him,——I'll only transport the Fellow——And so, Mr. *Catchpole,*—you may take him to *Newgate.*—

Gargle. Well, but, dear Sir, you know I always intended to marry my Daughter into your Family; and if you let the young Man be ruined, my Money must all go into another Chanel.—

Wingate. How's that!—into another Chanel!——Must not lose the handling of his Money——Why, I told you, Friend *Gargle,* I'm not a hard-hearted Man.——

Gargle. Why no, Sir—but your Passions—However, if you will but make the young Gentleman serve out the last Year of his Apprenticeship, you know I shall be giving over, and I may put him into all my Practice.—

G 2 *Wingate.*

* Romeo and Juliet,   † Barbarossa.

Wingate. Ha! ha!—Why—if the Block-head would but get as many crabbed physical Words from *Hyppocrites* and *Allen*, as he has from his nonsensical Trumpery,—ha! ha;—I don't know, between you and I, but he might pass for a very good Physician.—

Dick. * And must I leave thee, *Juliet?*—

Charlotte. Nay, but, prithee now have done with your Speeches——You see we are brought to the last Distress, and so you had better make it up—   [*Aside to* Dick.

Dick. Why, for your Sake, my Dear, I could almost find in my Heart—

Wingate. You'll settle your Money on your Daughter?—

Gargle. You know it was always my Intention.—

Wingate. I must not let the Cash slip thro' my Hands [*Aside*]: Look-ye here, young Man——I am the best-natured Man in the World——How came this Debt, Friend?

Bailiff. The Gentleman gave his Note at *Bristol*, I understands, where he boarded—'tis but Twenty Pounds.—

Wingate. Twenty Pounds! Well, why don't you send to your Friend *Shakespeare* now to bail you—ha! ha! I should like to see *Shakespeare* give Bail—ha! ha!—Mr. *Catchpole*, will you take Bail of *Ben Thompson*, and *Shakespeare* and *Odissy Popes?*—

Bailiff. No such People have been here, Sir—are they House-keepers?——

Dick. † You do not come to mock my Miseries?——

Gargle. Hush! young Man, you'll spoil all—Let me speak to you—How is your Digestion?
                                                   Dick.

* Romeo and Juliet.   † Mourning Bride.

Dick. * Throw Phyfic to the Dogs, I'll none of it——

Charlotte. Nay, but dear *Dick*, for my Sake--

Wingate. What fays he, *Gargle?*——

Gargle. He repents, Sir——he'll reform.——

Wingate. That's right, Lad—now you're right——and if you will but ferve out your Time, my Friend *Gargle* here will make a Man of you——Wounds! you'll have his Daughter and all his Money—And if I hear no more of your Trumpery, and you mind your Bufinefs, and ftick to my little *Charlotte*, and make me a Grandfather in my old Days,—Egad, you fhall have all mine too——that is, when I'm dead.——

Dick. Charlotte,—that will do rarely, and we may go to the Play as often as we pleafe—

Charlotte. O *Gemini*, it will be the pureft Thing in the World, and we'll fee *Romeo* and *Juliet* every Time it is acted.——

Dick. Ay, and that will be a hundred Times in a Seafon at leaft——Befides, it will be like a Play, if I reform at the End——† Sir, free me fo far in your moft generous Thoughts, that I have fhot my Arrow o'er the Houfe, and hurt my Brother——

Wingate. What do you fay, Friend?——

Charlotte. Nay, but prithee now do it in plain *Englifh*——

Dick. Well, well, I will——He knows nothing of Metaphors——Sir, you fhall find for the future, that we'll both endeavour to give you all the Satisfaction in our Power.——

Wingate. Very well, that's right——you may do very well——Friend *Gargle*, I'm overjoy'd——

Gargle.

* Macbeth.   † Hamlet.

Gargle. Chearfulnefs, Sir, is the principal Ingredient in the Compofition of Health.——

Wingate. Wounds! Man, let's hear no more of your Phyfick——Here, young Man, put this Book in your Pocket, and let me fee how foon you'll be Mafter of Vulgar Fractions.——Mr. *Catchpole*, ftep home with me, and I'll pay you the Money——you feem to be a notable Sort of a Fellow, Mr. *Catchpole*, ——could you nab a Man for me?

Catchpole. Faft enough, Sir, when I've the Writ——

Wingate. Very well, come along——I lent a young Gentleman a Hundred Pounds, ——a cool Hundred he call'd it——ha! ha!——it did not ftay to cool with him——I had a good Præmium; but I fha'n't wait a Moment for that——Come along, young Man;—— What Right have you to Twenty Pounds?— give you Twenty Pounds?——I never was obliged to my Family for Twenty Pounds— but I'll fay no more——if you have a Mind to thrive in this World, make yourfelf ufeful, is the *Golden Rule.*

Dick. My dear *Charlotte*, as you are to be my Reward, I will be a new Man——

Charlotte. Well, now I fhall fee how much you love me——

Dick. It fhall be my Study to deferve you— and fince we don't go on the Stage, 'tis fome Comfort that the World's a Stage, and all the Men and Women merely Players.

Some play the upper, fome the under Parts,
And moft affume what's foreign to their Hearts;
Thus, Life is but a Tragic-comic Jeft,
And all is Farce and Mummery at beft.

EPI-

E P I L O G U E,

Written by a F R I E N D.

Spoken by Mrs. C L I V E.

Enters reading the Play Bill.

A Very pretty Bill,—as I'm alive!
The Part of—Nobody——by Mrs. Clive !
A poltry, scribling Fool——to leave me out—
He'll say, perhaps—he thought I could not Spout.
Malice and Envy to the last Degree !
And why ?—I wrote a Farce as well as He.
And fairly ventur'd it, without the Aid
Of Prologue dress'd in Black, and Face in Masquerade ; }
O Pit—have Pity—see how I'm dismay'd !
Poor Soul !—this canting Stuff will never do,
Unless, like Boyes, he brings his Hangman too.
But granting that from these same Obsequies,
Some Pickings to our Bard in Black arise ;
Should your Applause to Joy convert his Fear,
As Pallas turns to Feast—Lardella's Bier ;
Yet 'twould have been a better Scheme by half
T'have thrown his Weeds aside, and learnt with me to
         laugh.
I could have shewn him, had he been inclin'd,
A spouting Junto of the Female Kind.
There dwells a Milliner in yonder Row,
Well dress'd, full voic'd, and nobly built for Shew,
Who, when in Rage, she scolds at Sue *and* Sarah,
Damn'd, Damn'd Dissembler !—thinks she's more than
    ZARA.
She has a Daughter too that dealt in Lace,
And sings—O ponder well—and Chevy Chase, }
And fain would fill the fair Ophelia's *Place.*

And

EPILOGUE.

And in her cock'd up Hat, and Gown of Camblet,
Presumes on something——touching the Lord Hamlet.
A Cousin too she has, with squinting Eyes,
With wadling Gait, and Voice like London Cries;
Who, for the Stage too short by half a Story,
Acts Lady Townly——thus——in all her Glory.
And, while she's traversing the scanty Room,
Cries——" Lord, my Lord, what can I do at home !"
In short, there's Girls enough for all the Fellows, ⎫
The Ranting, Whining, Starting, and the Jealous, ⎬
The Hotspurs, Romeos, Hamlets, and Othellos. ⎭
Oh ! little do these silly People know,
What dreadful Trials——Actors undergo.
Myself——who most in Harmony delight,
Am scolding here from Morning until Night.
Then take Advice from me, ye giddy Things,
Ye Royal Milliners, ye apron'd Kings ;
Young Men beware, and shun our slipp'ry Ways,
Study Arithmetic, and burn your Plays ;
And you, ye Girls, let not our Tinsel Train
Enchant your Eyes, and turn your madd'ning Brain ;
Be timely wise, for oh ! be sure of this !——
A Shop with Virtue is the Height of Bliss.

FINIS.